THINGS HAWAIIAN

A P...
GU...
TO THE HAWAIIAN
LANGUAGE

ISLAND HERITAGE

Contents

Introduction

Although your first glimpse of the Waikiki skyline shows a profile you might find in almost any resort city in the world, a closer look begins to reveal things that are uniquely Hawaiian. The most important of these is the language. You see it in the names of streets and hotels, and you hear it in songs, greetings, and the words borrowed into the informal brand of English spoken in Hawai'i. You can even find many Hawaiian words in English dictionaries, for we have borrowed the names of plants, birds, fish, and geological features unique to Hawai'i.

Hawaiian, like every other language, is more than just a tool for communication. It is a window that lets us look at the culture – one that may have changed dramatically with the introduction of so many competing ones, but one that still lives.

Many parts of this culture are reflected by the language –

how people deal with each other, what they eat, what they wear, how they spend their leisure time, what they name their children, how they celebrate special occasions, how they campaign for political office, what kinds of arts and crafts they create–all these things and many more.

If you're a visitor to this culture, it's often hard to participate in it, because you don't usually stay long enough to find out how things work. Even if you're *kamaʻāina* (born here, or long-term resident), there's so much outside influence that the real Hawaiian culture is sometimes hard to find.

But the language is the starting point. Even knowing a little bit about Hawaiian – especially how to pronounce it – will enrich your stay in the Islands by giving you a greater appreciation for the way people here live.

The Alphabet

Starting with Captain James Cook in 1778, many visitors to Hawai'i tried to write some of the Hawaiian words they heard, mostly the names of people, places, and unfamiliar customs, artifacts, flora, and fauna. But they all did it in their own way. For example, English speakers wrote the words according to the patterns of English spelling, but French, German, or Spanish speakers used their own systems. In other words, they all heard the language differently. This was only natural, for most of these people were short-term visitors with no chance to learn how the language really works. The result was that there was no one *correct* way to spell a Hawaiian word.

It was not until the 1820s, with the arrival of the New England missionaries (who realized that a written language was essential for education and Bible translation), that a standard alphabet began to develop. But it didn't happen overnight. Instead, it took about six years of questioning native speakers, consulting among themselves, and seeking advice from American and British scholars and missionaries in other parts of Polynesia.

The first thing the missionaries did to improve Hawaiian spelling was to replace the English way of writing vowel sounds with the so-called "continental" system, which was by this time used successfully for Tahitian and Māori, both close relatives of Hawaiian. Quite by accident, Hawaiian and other Polynesian languages have vowel systems much like that of Latin, so there was a perfect match between the vowel sounds and the letters available in the Roman alphabet:

a e i o u

Now, there was no need to spell Hawaiian vowels with such awkward English spellings as *ee, oo,* and *y*.

However, the consonants were much harder to deal with, for some of them varied from place to place and from speaker to speaker. Moreover, several of the sounds were so different from those of English that outsiders couldn't decide just what was being said. For example, one writer complained that he had seen the name *Kamehameha* (Hawai'i's most notable chief) spelled over a dozen ways.

Especially troublesome were the pairs **b–p, t–k, l–r,** and **v–w.** At first, all these letters were used. But it really made no difference which sound or letter you used. For instance, whether you said **tai** or **kai,** the word still meant 'sea'. In the same way, you could use either **lani** or **rani** for 'heaven', **vai** or **wai** for 'water'. And this held for any words containing these sounds.

How could the problem be solved? Keeping all the letters would have produced chaos. For example, how could anyone write a dictionary if most words could be spelled several ways?

Helped by the advice of the Hawaiians, the missionaries came up with this answer. Obviously, the extra letters weren't necessary. By deleting **b, t, r,** and **v,** they produced an alphabet that – with the addition of two extra symbols which you'll see below – satisfies the requirement for an ideal writing system: an exact match between letters and significant sounds.

By simplifying the alphabet, the missionaries didn't intend to change the language itself. As a matter of fact, you can still hear the **r** and **t** pronunciations in some places, and **v** is common all over Hawai'i, even though none of these letters is still written.

The revised system worked so well that teachers in the late 1820s proudly claimed that students could learn to be perfect readers and spellers in a month. This is still true today. If you hear a Hawaiian word, you can spell it. And if you see a word written, you can pronounce it.

But, as with any alphabet, you need a few guidelines. The next section shows you how to pronounce some of the many Hawaiian words you're bound to see here.

How to Pronounce Hawaiian

VOWELS

Here are the closest equivalents in English:

a : ah!
e : bait
i : beet
o : boat
u : boot

(These English examples are only a rough guide. Actually, Hawaiian has "pure" vowels – without the **w** or **y** sound that ends some of the English vowels.)

Some vowels fit together as units – that is, as diphthongs. Here is a complete list:

ai	ae	au	ao
ei	eu	oi	ou	iu

Each vowel can be either long or short. A long vowel is marked with the first of the extra symbols mentioned above – a **kahakō** (macron), or line over the vowel. This is how the long vowels are written:

ā   ē   ī   ō   ū

As you'd expect, a long vowel lasts longer than a short one. The following pairs of words show how important it is to mark long vowels:

kane skin disease
kāne male

ʻaina meal
ʻāina land

As you can see, lengthening a vowel changes the meaning of a word. There's a big difference between these two phrases: **aloha ʻāina** 'love of the land' and **aloha ʻaina** 'love of a meal'! For this reason, it's just as important to mark long vowels as it is to write a **p** or an **o**, or any other letter.

CONSONANTS

h	as in	**h**ouse
k	as in	s**k**in
l	as in	**l**ead
m	as in	**m**at
p	as in	s**p**in
n	as in	**n**o
w	as in	**w**ear/**v**ery
'	as in	oh-oh
		(between the oh's)

Two consonants take some extra practice. The first is the **'okina** (glottal stop), which is the second symbol that was later added to the alphabet. It isn't written with one of the usual letters of the Roman alphabet, but with a backward apostrophe: **'**.

Just like any other consonant, the **'okina** keeps pairs of words from being confused: for example, it's the only difference between **kou** 'your' and **ko'u** 'my'. Here are a few more examples:

mai	here
ma'i	sick
kai	sea
ka'i	to lead
nou	throw
no'u	mine

Next, **w** ranges from a [w] to a [v] sound, sometimes sounding like something between the two – rather like a v made with both lips. There are no strict rules to follow, except for a tendency to hear [w], rather than [v], after *o* or *u*. You'll have to listen to how native speakers pronounce this sound.

PUTTING CONSONANTS AND VOWELS TOGETHER

Hawaiian words are put together very differently from English words. You can never find two or more consonants together, and every syllable (and thus, every word) ends in a vowel. A syllable can be made up of just one vowel, and so some Hawaiian words can consist of vowels alone. An example is **ua** 'rain' (two syllables) or **uia**, a kind of taro (three syllables).

However, it's more common for a syllable to begin with a consonant. Here are some examples, divided into syllables: **ma-ha-lo** 'thank you', **ka-na-ka** 'person', **Ka-'a-'a-wa** (place name).

How do diphthongs fit into syllables? They make up just one syllable, not two. As you just saw, **ua** 'rain' is two syllables. But the same vowels in the reverse order form a diphthong: **au** 'I' is one syllable.

It's occasionally been suggested that because Hawaiian has a relatively small alphabet (five vowels and eight consonants), it couldn't have a very large vocabulary. Well, let's put this to the test. Including long vowels, diphthongs, and long diphthongs, the language has a potential for 225 one-syllable words. If we add two-, three-, and four-syllable words, the figure rises to:

2,574,332,100

That's more than enough for any language!

ACCENT: PUTTING SYLLABLES TOGETHER

Whenever you hear two or three syllables together, one is more prominent than the others. This is called *accent*. Many languages don't mark accent, and Hawaiian is no exception. But still, it's important for correct pronunciation.

For shorter words, accent is predictable: You hear it on the second-to-last vowel, or on any long vowel or diphthong. For example, **máka** 'eye', **mahálo** 'thank you', **kū́** 'stand', **kái** 'sea', **Ka'ū́** (an area on the island of Hawai'i). Note that in the word **kái**, which contains a diphthong, the accent is on the first vowel. This is always the case, no matter where the diphthong appears in a word.

In terms of accent, longer words are made by putting these units together. For example, the name **Waikīkī** 'spouting water' has one diphthong and two long vowels. Thus it has three accent units and is pronounced:

Wái.kí.kí

with three "beats" – the last

stronger than the others. As another example, take the name of the voyaging canoe, **Hōkūle'a** ('joyous star'). It is pronounced:

Hó.kú.lé'a

Finally, the name of a major street in Honolulu (leading to the Ala Moana Shopping Center), **Ke'eaumoku**, is pronounced:

Ké'e.áu.móku

Except for most place names, you can find the pronunciation of longer words in the latest *Hawaiian Dictionary*, in which these units are separated by periods. Normally, words aren't spelled this way, but in the lists below, words are divided into smaller pieces to show you how they are accented. And now that you know where the accents are in these small units, we don't have to use accent marks.

Common Hawaiian Words and Phrases

PLACE NAMES

Whether you're a resident or a visitor, you're almost sure to use place names in your conversations. After all, how can you enjoy Hawai'i without talking about the places you've seen?

Here, you can learn how to pronounce some of the most common names and avoid the usual mistakes: ignoring the glottal stop and long vowels, and pronouncing the vowels as if they were English.

First, the island names (remember that the periods mark accent units):

Hawai'i
Kaho'o.lawe
Kau.a'i
Lā.na'i
Maui
Molo.ka'i
Ni'i.hau
O'ahu

You can see that Maui is the only island name without a glottal stop. For the other names, be sure to use the glottal stop in the right places. Remember, it's just like any other consonant.

Here's the proper pronunciation of some street and area names that are often mispronounced:

     Haʻi.kū
     Kalā.kaua
     Kapiʻo.lani
     Keʻe.au.moku
     Kū.hiō

Lā.ʻie
Li.hu.ʻe
Mā.noa
Kameha.meha
Kāne.ʻohe
Mā.kaha
Mō.ʻili.ʻili
Puna.luʻu
Wai.ʻalae
Hale.maʻu.maʻu
Wahi.awā
Wai.kī.kī
Wai.ʻanae

In the name **Hono.lulu**,
it's the vowels that are often
wrong. Speakers of English
tend to pronounce the first one
'*ah*' and the second and last
ones '*uh*'. Instead, the first two
should have a real '*oh*' sound,
and the next two the *u* sound
in *rude*.

GREETINGS AND COMMON PHRASES

Here are some expressions that many people know, even if they aren't fluent speakers of Hawaiian. Try them!

'Ae.	Yes.
A hui hou.	Goodbye.
A hui hou aku.	Goodbye (response).
Aloha.	Hello, goodbye (also *love*).
'A'ole.	No.
'A'ole pili.kia.	You're welcome (lit., no trouble).
E hele mai.	Come!
E kala mai ia'u.	Pardon me.
E komo mai.	Come in.
E 'olu.'olu 'oe.	Please.
Hau.'oli Maka.hiki Hou!	Happy New Year!
Mahalo.	Thank you.
Mahalo nui loa.	Thank you very much.
Mele Kaliki.maka!	Merry Christmas!
'Ono loa!	Really delicious!
Ua pau.	Finished.

DIRECTIONS

ma kai toward the sea
ma uka inland, toward mountains
(pronounced **máuka**)

Many people who live in Hawai'i use these words, rather than compass directions, in their English.

NUMBERS

'ekahi	one	'eono	six
'elua	two	'ehiku	seven
'ekolu	three	'ewalu	eight
'ehā	four	'eiwa	nine
'elima	five	'umi	ten

The higher numbers work this way:

11-19: **'umi.kū.mā.kahi**, etc.

20: **iwa.kā.lua**

21-29: **iwa.kā.lua.kū.mā.kahi**, etc.

30: **kana.kolu**

40: **kana.hā**

50: **kana.lima**

60: **kana.ono**, etc.

See if you can write the Hawaiian words for these numbers, using the patterns above. The answers are on page 59.

15 —————————————

26 —————————————

38 —————————————

42 —————————————

65 —————————————

The words **hapa** 'half', **hanele** 'hundred', **kau.kani** 'thousand', and **mili.ona** 'million' were borrowed from English.

CULTURAL WORDS

Here are just a few words that reflect Hawaiian culture. Again, they're often used in English as well.

ahu.pua'a	land division from uplands to the sea
hā.lau	place of instruction
haole	foreigner, Caucasian
hei.au	ancient temple
ho'o.lau.le'a	celebration
huki.lau	pull-net fishing
hula	dance with chant
kā.hili	feather standard
kahuna	priest, expert
kama.'āina	native, long-time resident

kapa	barkcloth
kule.ana	responsibility, right
kumu	teacher
lei	garland
lo'i	irrigated terrace for taro
maka.hiki	year, a festival
mana	supernatural power
mele	song
Mene.hune	mythical (?) small people
mō.'i	sovereign
'ohana	family
oli	chant without an accompanying dance
Pele	volcano goddess

FOOD

Sampling exotic food is one of our favorite ways of participating in a new culture. Most of the following foods are traditional, but some have a slight mixture of other cultures as well. First, here are some names for the occasions you might have to try the foods.

lū.ʻau	feast
baby lū.ʻau	party to celebrate a child's first birthday
pā.ʻina	meal, dinner, dinner party
ʻaha.ʻaina	feast or banquet

And here are some ways of cooking food:

imu earth oven

Food that is cooked in an imu is described as:

kā.lua pit-cooked

Another method is:

huli.huli rotisseried.

This kind of cooking is a favorite fundraiser, and marinated chicken is the usual fare.

THE MENU

hau.pia	cold coconut cream pudding
huli.huli	rotisseried (e.g., chicken)
i'a	fish
kalo	taro
kā.lua (pork)	pork or other meat cooked in a pit
kō	sugarcane
kū.lolo	taro and coconut cream pudding
lau.lau	steamed taro-leaf-wrapped food
lili.ko'i	passion fruit
limu	seaweed
lomi.lomi salmon	minced salmon, tomato, onion
lū.'au	cooked taro leaves
mai'a	banana
mana.pua	Chinese pork cake
mea 'ai	food
moa	chicken
niu	coconut
'ono	delicious
pia	arrowroot
poha	cape gooseberry
poi	taro paste

poke	marinated raw fish
pua'a	pig
pū.pū	hors d'oeuvre
'uala	sweet potato
uhi	yam
'ulu	breadfruit

Here are the names of fish, shellfish, and other sea creatures that are commonly eaten in Hawai'i:

'ahi	yellowfin tuna
aku	ocean bonito or skip jack
akule	scad fish
a'u	swordfish, sailfish, marlin, spearfish

honu	turtle
kā.hala	amberjack
kawa.kawa	bonito
mahi.mahi	dolphin-fish
ʻō.ʻio	bonefish, used for fish cake
ʻō.paka.paka	snapper
ʻō.pelu	mackerel scad
ʻopihi	limpet
ulua	crevalle, a game and table fish
walu	oilfish
wana	sea urchin
manō	shark

CONDIMENTS

pa'a.kai	salt
kō.pa'a	sugar
pinika	vinegar
mā.keke	mustard
nī.oi	chili pepper

DRINKS

kī	tea
kope	coffee
pia	beer
wai	(fresh) water
mai.tai	rum, fruit juice drink
'ō.kole.hao	ti-root liquor
wai lemi	lemonade
wai.ū	milk

This is how to ask for one of these foods or drinks:

**E 'olu'olu 'oe,
makemake au i ka _____.
(pa'a.kai, wai, poi** etc.)

Please, I'd like some _____.
(salt, water, poi, etc.).

Of course, because it's been influenced by so many cultures and languages from the outside, Hawaiian has borrowed many words for food and drink. One of the earliest of these, from 1810, was **tabete** (as it was spelled then) 'cabbage'. And **meli** 'honey' comes from Greek, introduced by the missionaries.

But most of the words were borrowed from English. See if you can guess the meaning of these words for food or drink (the answers are on page 59):

1.	kū.lina	9.	lā.paki
2.	weke.kē	10.	lama
3.	ʻalani	11.	kali.palaoa
4.	lekuke	12.	pelena
5.	kā.mano	13.	pī
6.	laiki	14.	pia
7.	kamako	15.	lemi
8.	waina	16.	pipi

Here's a handy phrase you can use after sampling all these foods:
   Mā.ʻana! or **Mā.ʻona!**   I'm full!

CLOTHING

holo.kū	gown with a train
malo	loincloth
muʻu.muʻu	full-length Hawaiian dress
palaka	checkered shirt (Eng. *frock*)
pā.pale	hat
pā.ū	sarong

FLOWERS, TREES, AND OTHER PLANTS

'ape	elephant ears (large taro-like plant)
'awa.puhi	ginger
hala	pandanus
hau	type of hibiscus
'ilima	a shrub with delicate yellow flowers: O'ahu's official *lei.*
kā.hili ginger	ginger with cluster of blossoms shaped like a *kā.hili*
kiawe	Algaroba tree, a legume
kī	ti plant *(Cordyline terminalis)*
koa	native *Acacia*, reddish hardwood
kukui	candlenut tree
lehua (**'ō.hi'a**)	red flower of the *'ō.hi'a*: the island of Hawai'i's official flower

limu	seaweed, any water plant
loke.lani	red rose: Maui's official flower
maile	native twining shrub whose vine is used for *lei*
mauna.loa	a vine whose flowers are used for *lei*
moki.hana	native tree whose fruits are used for Kaua'i's official *lei*
noni	Indian mulberry once used for dyes and medicine
olo.nā	native shrub whose bark is used for fiber
pī.kake	jasmine
wauke	paper mulberry, used for *kapa*
wili.wili	tree with light wood, once used for surfboards and fishnet floats

BIRDS

'apa.pane	red and black honey creeper
'ele.paio	sp. flycatcher
mamo	black honey creeper
nē.nē	Hawaiian goose (State bird)
'ō.'ō.'ā.'ā	Kaua'i sp. of honey eater
'ō.'ū	Honey creeper with green feathers
pueo	Hawaiian short-eared owl

ANIMALS

hipa	sheep
lio	horse
hoke	mule
moa	fowl
'ī.lio	dog
pō.poki	cat
'iole	rat
pua'a	pig
kao	goat

GENERAL

'a'ā	rough lava
akamai	smart
hana	work
hana hou	Encore!
hā.nai	adopted
hā.pai	pregnant
hau.'oli	happy
he'e nalu	go surfing
hiki.e'e	large couch
huhū	angry
kai	sea
kama.'āina	native, longtime resident

kāne	male, man
kapu	taboo
keiki	child
kō.kua	help
kolohe	naughty
kū.kū	grandparent (usually **tū.tū**)
kupuna	grandparent, source
lā.nai	terrace, porch
lō.lō	stupid
lomi.lomi	massage
lua	toilet
luna	boss
mai.kaʻi	good
mali.hini	visitor
moana	sea
nī.ele	curious
noa	free from kapu
pā.hoe.hoe	smooth lava
pali	cliff
pani.olo	cowboy *(español)*
pau	finished
pau hana	quitting time
pilau	rotten, dirty
pili.kia	trouble

polo.lei	upright, right
puka	hole
pū.neʻe	movable couch
pupule	crazy
ʻuku.lele	ukulele
wahine	female, woman
wiki.wiki	fast

O-Things and A-Things: A World View

One of the unusual features of Hawaiian (and of most Polynesian languages, for that matter) is the way the language reflects the culture's attitude toward possessions. In English, the system is fairly simple: we say **my** *hand*, **my** *father*, **my** *car*, **my** *child*, **my** *book*, **my** *fish*, **my** *picture*, and so on. But in Hawaiian, the first three concepts use one kind of "my," the next three another, and the last either kind, depending on the specific meaning. Here's how it works.

There are two complete sets of possessive words (equivalents of English *my, your, her, his,* etc.). They differ only in the accented vowel: one set has **o**, the other has **a**.

The difference between the two classes depends on the relationship between the possessor and the thing possessed. Take the examples above. First, **my** *hand*. This is a relationship that I can neither start nor stop. In other words, I can't control it. The same is true for **my** *father*.

Hawaiian expresses this relationship by using **o** in the possessive: thus, *ko'u lima* 'my hand', *ko'u makua.kāne* 'my father'.

Thus, a possessive word with a body part name or a relative at the same level as the speaker (brother, sister, cousin) or above (parents, grandparents) takes **o**.

Most Polynesian languages follow this general principle. But individual languages vary in details. Hawaiian extends the **o** category to include clothing and structures that you can enter or ride upon – in a sense, extensions of one's body. Thus, **ko'u malo** 'my loincloth', **ko'u wa'a** 'my canoe', **ko'u hale** 'my house'. Here are some more examples of **o**-forms:

> **kou kū.puna**
> your grandparents
> **kou maka**
> your face, eye
> **kou po'o**
> your head
> **kona makua.hine**
> his, her mother

This is how the a category works. For items such as a book or a fish, the owners control whether or not they have them. And relatives below our level *(child, grandchild)* take possessive words with **a**. Thus, *ka'u keiki* 'my child', *ka'u puke* 'my book', *ka'u i'a* 'my fish'.

Finally, with some words, two meanings are possible, depending on whether **o** or **a** is used. Take **ki'i** 'picture', for example. If it's a picture *of* me – that is, a painting or photograph of me, it's **ko'u ki'i**. But if it's simply a picture that I own, then it's **ka'u ki'i**. See how this fits the pattern? Even if I give "my likeness" away, it's still my picture. The word **lei** works the same way. **Ko'u lei** 'my lei' is one that someone has given to me – an honor, and something very important culturally. I don't control the fact that it's "mine." But **ka'u lei** is one that I've made – of little cultural importance until I bestow it on someone else.

If you want to say 'my'

and avoid choosing between **a** and **o**, you can use the form **ku'u**. But this often carries an affectionate connotation as well:

> **ku 'u ipo** my sweetheart
> **ku 'u lei** my child (here
> *lei* is a metaphor)

Of course, this explanation has been oversimplified somewhat. But it illustrates how language can give us a view into a culture, revealing how people think and feel about things.

Hawaiian's Past

Hawaiian, along with about thirty other languages, belongs to the Polynesian family, which is spread over a large part of the Pacific Ocean. Within this family, Hawaiian seems closest to Tahitian, Māori, and Marquesan, less so to Samoan, and much less so to Tongan. Hawaiian is also related (but more distantly) to many languages further west – including those spoken in Fiji, Indonesia, the Philippines, and Madagascar.

In spite of the famous Kon-Tiki voyage from Peru to French Polynesia in 1947, which showed that it was *possible* to sail to the islands from the east, the main migrations to Polynesia were almost certainly from the opposite direction. As for the settlement of Hawai'i, some theories name the Marquesas Islands as one of the sources, and from A.D. 930 to 1300 as a possible range of dates. But stay tuned! Researchers keep finding new evidence that pushes the dates further back!

Polynesian languages share many features. The following list of common words, for example, shows you how similar at least part of the vocabulary is:

Hawaiian	Tahitian	Māori	English
ahi.ahi	ahi.ahi	ahi.ahi	evening
hale	fare	whare	house
inu	inu	inu	drink
koko	toto	toto	blood
lele	rere	rere	fly
lima	rima	ringa	hand
maka	mata	mata	face, eye
manu	manu	manu	bird
moe	moe	moe	sleep
muli	muri	muri	behind
niho	niho	niho	tooth
ola	ora	ora	live
wa'a	va'a	waka	canoe
wahine	vahine	wahine	woman

This similarity shows why early explorers thought they were all dialects of the "Polynesian language." However, there are many differences as well, and for the most part, it takes some time for speakers of even the most closely related languages to come to understand each other.

Hawaiian's
Future

In the last few decades of the 19th century, a number of conditions combined to reduce the number of schools conducted in Hawaiian from 150 with 4078 students in 1880, to only one school with 26 students in 1897, and none in 1902. Even though educational policy did not immediately stifle the language, by discouraging its use among children, it had the effect of cutting it off at the roots. As a result, after only one generation, both Hawaiians and outsiders noted that younger speakers were not using the language properly, and some writers predicted that the next generation would know little else but English.

As the years went by, even though the language was still spoken, the average age of native speakers continued to rise. In the 1930s, Hawaiian was taught as a subject in some high schools and at the university, but the range of offerings was small. By the 1950s and

1960s it was thought that the language would survive only in place names, written texts, songs, and words borrowed into other languages.

Recently, however, a revival of interest in language and culture has given new life to Hawaiian. The most important outgrowths of this renaissance are immersion programs, ranging from the preschool to the high school level, in which all subjects are taught in Hawaiian.

But no language can survive without culture. There has also been a growing interest in hula (especially through instruction and performances of **nā hā.lau** 'hula schools'), shipbuilding and voyaging (through the **Hō.kū.le'a** and other traditional craft), the martial arts (**lua**), and herbal healing (**lā.'au lapa.'au**). In these activities, language and culture work hand in hand, giving people opportunities to gather and speak Hawaiian in a natural context. Thus, arts and crafts supplement language classes, all helping to breathe new life into a highly endangered language.

Here are the answers to the quiz on words for food borrowed from English (p. 38):

1. corn
2. whiskey
3. orange
4. lettuce
5. salmon
6. rice
7. tomato
8. wine
9. rabbit
10. rum
11. cauliflower
12. bread
13. pea
14. beer
15. lemon
16. beef

And here's how to write those numbers (p. 29):

15 'umikūmālima
26 iwakāluakūmāono
38 kanakolukūmāwalu
42 kanahākūmālua
65 kanaonokūmālima

FURTHER READING

If this sketch of Hawaiian has whetted your appetite for more, try the following books, all published by the University of Hawai'i Press.

All About Hawaiian.
    Albert J. Schütz.
The Voices of Eden: A History of Hawaiian Language Studies.
    Albert J. Schütz.
Hawaiian Dictionary.
    Mary Kawena Pukui
    and Samuel H. Elbert.
New Pocket Hawaiian Dictionary.
    Mary Kawena Pukui
    and Samuel H. Elbert.
Pocket Place Names of Hawai'i.
    Mary Kawena Pukui,
    Samuel H. Elbert,
    and Esther T. Mookini.

PAU (THIS MEANS 'FINISHED'!)